A Dazzling
Display of Dogs

A
Dazzling
Display
of Dogs

Concrete poems by Betsy Franco

Illustrations by Michael Wertz

Tricycle Press
Berkeley

All rights reserved. Published in the United States by
Tricycle Press, an imprint of Random House Children's
Books, a division of Random House, Inc., New York.
www.randomhouse.com/kids

Tricycle Press and the Tricycle Press colophon are
registered trademarks of Random House, Inc.

Library of Congress Cataloging-in-Publication Data

Franco, Betsy.
  A dazzling display of dogs / by Betsy Franco.
      p. cm.
  1. Dogs--Juvenile poetry. 2. Concrete poetry, American. 3.
Children's poetry, American. I. Title.
  PS3556.R3325D39 2011
  811'.54--dc22

                        2010018014

ISBN 978-1-58246-343-8 (hardcover)
ISBN 978-1-58246-387-2 (Gibraltar lib. bdg.)

Printed in Malaysia

Design by Nancy Austin and Katy Brown
Typeset in Adrianna
The illustrations in this book were started in pencil and
finished using monoprints and Adobe Photoshop.

1 2 3 4 5 6 – 16 15 14 13 12 11

First Edition

ACKNOWLEDGMENTS

For Speedy, Takako, Buster, Dave the Dog, Miss Olive, Bones, Mack, Jack, Perkins, Pepita, Dino, Sam, Jake, Sara, Domino, Baloo, Hobee, Emmett, Tonka, Tigger, Bodie, Mollie, Sage, Maggie, Jazz, Phoebe, Fast Eddie, Ethan, Jockey, Merry Margaret, Farley, Siddharth, Trixie, Misha, Ben, Barry, Bandit, Darla and Steve, Pepper Ann, Maddy, Sirius Black, Bubba, Bailey, Joey, Kaia, Valentine, Reedy, Lady, and Little.

Thank you to all my family members, neighbors, friends, and Ms. Mason's students for their delightful dog stories.

Lastly, thank you to the two poets who inspired the style of two poems: bpNichol for "Salt Water Mutt" and Bob Grumman for "Missing."
—B.F.

First and foremost, I'd like to send love and dedicate these pictures to my husband, Andy, whose unwavering support allows me to continue making my art. Love to Miss Olive for changing our lives (for the better) forever. Thanks to the Berkeley Animal Shelter for finding Miss Olive, and thanks to Cameron at *Bark Magazine* for encouraging us to stick with a rambunctious pit mix. Thanks to my Mom who started me on my path, and brought us our childhood dogs, Golda and Misha. Thanks to my friends and family for patiently letting me hole up monk-like while I worked on this book, and thank you for buying a copy of this book from your local bookstore.
—M.W.

MY PAL, JAZZY

NO
MATTER
IF
I'M
FEELING
BLUE,
MY
JAZZY THINKS
I'M
GREAT.

SHE WIGGLES, JIGGLES, JUMPS ON ME WHEN I WALK THROUGH THE GATE!

FAST AL, THE RETIRED GREYHOUND

HE USED TO BE A RACING DOG, WHO RAN AROUND A TRACK. SO WHEN I TAKE HIM TO THE BEACH, HE WON'T RUN UP AND BACK. INSTEAD HE RUNS IN OVALS—HE'S ASTONISHINGLY FAST! HE WANTS TO WIN A RACE JUST LIKE HE USED TO IN THE PAST!

A SWOOSH OF SEAGULLS TEASES MY YAPPING DOG.
WHEN THEY LAND IN A CLUSTER,
HE CHARGES AND BARKS,
CHASING THEM, CHASING THEIR SHADOWS,
WISHING HE'D SPROUT WINGS.

TOUGH BERT

BERT THE MUTT'S A TOUGH OLD GUY.

HE'S HAD A LONG CAREER.

SCARS ON HIS NOSE.

MISSING CLAWS.

NICKS ON ONE OF HIS EARS.

BALDING SPOT ON ONE BACK LEG.

NO WHISKERS ON THE RIGHT.

HE STRUTS AROUND
LIKE HE OWNS THE PARK,
AND HE'S EARNED IT
WITH EVERY FIGHT.

PUG APPEAL

IT'S ALMOST IMPOSSIBLE
NOT TO HUG
AND SAY SOMETHING SILLY
TO FRANK THE

MISLEADING SIGN

BEWARE of DOG

BUT
WILLY
RARELY
EVER
GROWLS

THAT HARMLESS
BEAGLE ONLY
YOOOOOWLS!

EMMETT'S ODE TO HIS TENNIS BALL

SLOBBERY, SLOPPY, SLIMY SPHERE—OH, TENNIS BALL, I HOLD YOU DEAR. YOU BOUNCE, I BOUND UP IN THE AIR. WE MAKE THE MOST INSEPARABLE PAIR.

JAKE THE JACK RUSSELL TERRIER

WOOFING AT BOBO,

GROWLING AT BRETT—

HE HASN'T BEEN FRIGHTENED BY ANY DOG YET.

NO MATTER IF POOCHES ARE MUSCLEY AND MEAN.

JAKE IS A PLUCKY LIL' BARKING MACHINE.

OLD LOTTIE ON A WALK

She stumbles out the open door, walks round the block, but not much more. She greets a dog who's just as slow, avoids a puppy on the go. She smells dry leaves, and then she pees on bushes or the nearest trees. She totters home, lies down and groans. That's quite enough for her old bones.

BUBBLES
MY SOCKS ARE RARELY SLIMY,
AND EACH ONE HAS A MATCH.
WHY? BECAUSE PETUNIA NOW
HAS BUBBLES SHE CAN SNATCH!
HER TEETH MAKE CLICKITY-CLACKING SOUNDS.
BOUNDS UP IN THE
CATCHES
BUT, DOESN'T SEEM TO CARE!

CRAZY COMBO

THE NEIGHBOR'S DOG, PENELOPE,
IS THE WEIRDEST MIX YOU'LL EVER SEE,
'CAUSE SHE'S A COMBO-DOG SURPRISE:

GERMAN SHEPHERD

DACHSHUND

A SHEPA DOX!

SHE TAKES THE PRIZE!

LABRA DOODLE

LABRADOR
+
POODLE

POM CHI

POMERANIAN
+
CHIHUAHUA

POOCHI

POODLE + CHIHUAHUA

MALTIPOO

MALTESE + POODLE

WHEN LUCY THE CAT CAME TO MY HOME

WHEN I SAW THAT SQUIRT
WAS HERE TO STAY,

THAT SHE CERTAINLY WASN'T
GOING AWAY,

I CONCLUDED WE HAD TO
COHABITATE,

AND THE THING TO DO WAS

C**OO**PERATE!

(ON COLD, DARK NIGHTS
HER PURRING'S GREAT!)

SHE DIDN'T BARK OR MAKE A FUSS. SHE WAGGED HER TAIL AND SMILED AT US.

SHE TROTTED OUT, CAME STRAIGHT TO ME, BECAME A PART OF MY FAMILY!

MATHILDA TRIED TO BITE IT OFF. SHE BATTED IT WITH HER PAWS. BUT NOTHING MADE A DENT IN IT—NOT EVEN SHARP WHITE CLAWS. NO, NOTHING COULD REMOVE THE THING, NOT EVEN SHARP WHITE CLAWS. ON MORNING WALK SHE MET MAURICE, WHO SAW THINGS WERE AMISS, BUT COULDN'T SHOW HIS SYMPATHY WITH A SLOPPY BOXER KISS. OH, HE COULDN'T EVEN REACH HER WITH A SLOPPY BOXER KISS.

LETTING GWEN IN AND OUT

IN AND OUT
IN AND OUT
GOES MY BASSETT GWEN.
I'M UP I'M DOWN.
I'M UP I'M DOWN.
I DO HER BIDDING WHEN
SHE FLAPS HER EARS
AND BEGS TO BE
LET IN AND OUT AGAIN...

AND AGAIN AND AGAIN
AND AGAIN AND AGAIN
AND AGAIN AND AGAIN.
AND AGAIN.

LICKING, SHIFTING, BREATHING, WHEEZING.
SNUFFLING, DROOLING, GUFFLING, SNEEZING.
DREAMING, Whimpering, TWITCHING, SNORING,
(SLEEPING WITH BROWNIE is never BORING).

AND WITH EXTRA-SPECIAL SPUNK AND GLEE, HE CHASES LILAC UP A TREE.

THE WORDS WAFFLE HEARS

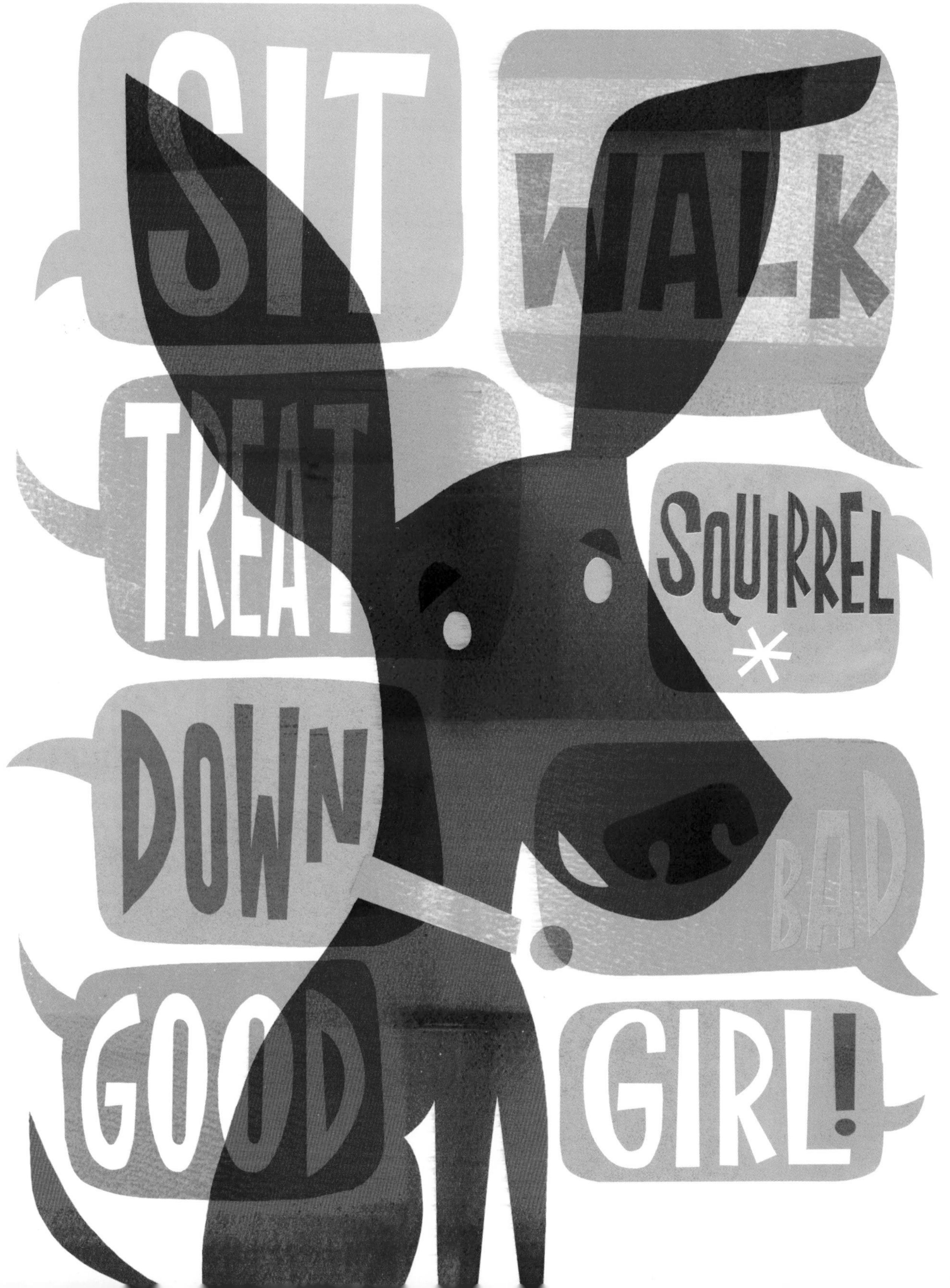

CIRCLING POEM I
PERKINS'S TAIL

PERKINS

PANTING

PERSISTENTLY

PURSUES

PUPPY TAIL

POLKA-DOTTED

SHE CIRCLES FOR THE PERFECT SPOT, BECAUSE SHE SIMPLY KNOWS SHE'S GOT TO FIND EXACTLY WHERE TO FLOP. SO ROUND SHE GOES, AND DOESN'T DROP UNTIL, AT LAST, SHE FINALLY STOPS. SHE LOOKS AROUND AND DOWN SHE PLOPS.

PIERRE PEEKS OUT

HE TRAVELS WITH ME
EVERYWHERE,
MY PEKINESE
PIERRE.
MY PUPPY FITS
INSIDE MY PACK
WITH LOTS OF
ROOM TO
SPARE.

DOG HAIKU

LABRADOR PUPPY
PIDDLES ON THE DAILY POST—
SUCH WATERED-DOWN NEWS.

THE CHAIR WITH THE RUFFLY TRIM WAS ALWAYS OFF LIMITS TO JIM, TILL HE CHEWED IT TO BITS, MADE IT THREADBARE WITH SLITS— NOW NO ONE SITS ON IT BUT HIM.

TONKA AT DOG SCHOOL

WITH ALL THE POOCHES AND THE SCENTS, THE DOGGY SCHOOL CAN BE INTENSE.

THE TEACHER'S TONE IS NO-NONSENSE.

MY LITTLE TONKA CAN BE DENSE.

IT MAKES HIM FEEL PRETTY TENSE

WHEN HE GETS CALLED FOR EACH OFFENSE...

'CAUSE HE LOVES THE COMPLIMENTS. BUT...

MY TONKA'S LEARNED OBEDIENCE.

HE REFUSES TO WEAR HIS WHITE TUTU. HE GLOWERS AND TURNS UP HIS NOSE. BUT HE BRINGS US HIS TURTLENECK SWEATER. MILO ONLY WEARS FASHIONABLE CLOTHES.

TIGGER ON HIS BACK

(A POEM FOR TWO VOICES)

SCRITCH ME.
SCRATCH
ME.

THUMP, THUMP,
THUMPITY-THUMP

PAT ME.
RUB ME.

THUMP, THUMP,
BUMPITY-BUMP

ITCH ME.
WATCH MY

THUMP, THUMP, THUMPITY-
THUMP

BACK LEG
JUMPING.

THUMP,
THUMP,
BUMPITY-BUMP

TWITCHING,
BUMPING,

THUMP, THUMP, THUMPITY-THUMP

THUMPITY-

THUMPITY-
BUMPITY

THUMPING.

THUMPITY-THUMP

TIGGER ON HIS BELLY
KNEAD MY EARS AND SCRATCH MY MUZZLE. IN RETURN, I'LL GIVE A NUZZLE.
STROKE ME UP AND DOWN MY SPINE. HEAR ME SING MY HAPPY WHINE.

THE TAIL END

WHENEVER I LET AMELIA OUT, I'M CAREFUL AND I'M SLOW, 'CAUSE AS SHE'S GOING OUT THE DOOR, HER TAIL'S THE LAST TO GO.